D0323321

# Man Living on a Side Creek
## and Other Poems

*Elmer Holmes Bobst Awards for Emerging Writers*

Established in 1983, the Elmer Holmes Bobst Awards in Arts and Letters are presented each year to individuals who have brought true distinction to the American literary scene. Recipients of the Awards include writers as varied as Toni Morrison, John Updike, Russell Baker, Eudora Welty, Edward Albee, Arthur Miller, Joyce Carol Oates, and James Merrill. The Awards were recently expanded to include categories devoted to emerging writers of poetry and fiction, and in 1993 the jurors selected winners in each category, Anne Marsella for her collection of short stories, *The Lost and Found and Other Stories*, and Stephan Torre for his collection of poems, *Man Living on a Side Creek and Other Poems*.

STEPHAN TORRE

# Man Living on a Side Creek and Other Poems

NEW YORK
UNIVERSITY PRESS
*New York and London*

NEW YORK UNIVERSITY PRESS
New York and London

Library of Congress Cataloging-in-Publication Data

Torre, Stephan.
Man living on a side creek and other poems / Stephan Torre.
p.   cm.
ISBN 0-8147-8207-8. — ISBN 0-8147-8208-6 (pbk.)
I. Title.
PS3570.0689M36   1994
811'.54—dc20          93-48473
                              CIP


Book design: Kathleen Szawiola


New York University Press books are printed on
acid-free paper, and their binding materials are chosen for strength
and durability.

Manufactured in the United States of America

10   9   8   7   6   5   4   3   2   1

*For my daughters, Colleen and Aeron,*
*who keep the horses smart,*
*and the owls awake*

*We ate the fish.*

—James Wright

# Contents

## III

## IV

# Acknowledgments

Grateful acknowledgment is made to the editors of the following publications in which some of these poems first appeared:

*American Poetry Review, Bloomsbury Review, The Dragonfly, Estero, Floating Island, Grain, Horsetails, The Malahat Review, Mānoa, Midnight Lamp, Poetry Northwest, Prairie Fire, Puerto del Sol, National Poetry Competition Anthology, Sonoma Mandala, The Southern Poetry Review, Transfer, Willow Springs,* and *Zyzzyva.*

# Man Living on a Side Creek
## and Other Poems

I

# The Sinker: Navarro Journal

I remember how we balanced on the springboard
with our axes, how the chips soared
past Boonville and San Francisco . . .
I remember the song of the misery whip,
the taste of good steel, how our shoulders
watered the sawdust.
The clear acid of that morning
sank through my body
like the blood of alders and suckers,
the osprey's salty claw . . .

       I remember
dogging the endless chain, yelling at the mules,
deep ruts through the ferns,
smoke and groaning oxen . . .
I was coiling rope and cranking the jack
as they crushed hillsides rolling into the river.
I remember farmers who spent their whole lives
feeding smoldering stumps, their sheep
biting red clay . . .
I stoked the steam donkey, leaping with sparks
as the huge cable tightened, gutting the darkness.

I danced on the mill pond
like Ahab (a banana slug clinging to my boot!)
I remember the grunting
as we canted the shaggy giant off the skidway
and drove in the dogs, dog teeth in my liver
as we tore into the purple old growth: the Sinker,
the Blue One . . . headsaw singing,

thunder of the carriage, slabs of gigantic meat,
our eyes all bloodshot with happiness,
the glowing mountain of bonemeal
against the blue sea—
salt lips of a motherless morning.

Cool odor of crushed fruit, sawdust
like a blast of wheat
through my ribs . . . I remember
the pit of silence
when the smokestack guttered, the flatbelts
and rollers whined still, and I saw the sun
standing in a pool of ravens.

I remember the stain on the brakeman's suspenders,
the harness of the white gelding
on the loading dock, the beautiful slime
of the pilings, the small wrists of the mill-owner's wife.
I remember the schooner plowing in
through unbelievable rocks and foam,
the red grin of the captain . . .

## Headland Farm

The tractor rusts like a lizard
in the foggy thistles.

Horse harness rots off its spike
in the windy shed.

Cattle scratch their lice under the eaves
until the gray house collapses.

A hawk chops out of the mist . . .

What did they want
of this red clay, seacoast
bulging with birds and deep grass?

His back to the sun, he drove pickets
down to the edge of the headland.
His face burned like plough steel
and morning smoked in his footsteps.

What did they want, turning the meadow
over and over, until the barn filled
with ocean, and the moon sank
in the cellar?

Berries blackened at the sill.
Her face tightened against the wind, her voice
blew out like chaff.

Season by season they became
strangers to the sea
and to each other.

A man pushes himself
until the land warps
like the boards he loved.

Pushes until bitterness has carved his hand
into a root that holds
a rusty cup, and he has forgotten
that he was thirsty, or in love.

# In Praise of Rain

The storm has pushed me
inside again, thank god.

Enough dry wood to keep the tea hot,
acorns thumping on the roof.

Beneath the gas light an oak moth
is laying her eggs in an open book.

It is November. This fist making words
has darkened like a manzanita root.

# Water Calling

A Kootenai waded naked
in my childhood, an osprey
dropped a rainbow
in my mouth.

Ben Walker took me with him
and a bag of cherries,
dipping cold water
into a wooden barrel.

He made me hold the reins
going home, tanned me
a buffalo's forehead,
believe it or not,

and I have lost it . . .
but not the knife
in my leg pocket with fish
scales for nearly thirty years.

My room was "The Tower"
above the boathouse
and the worm box, my green
window full of stones.

Grandma waved from the dock
and let me troll alone
from Devils Slide to Big Arm,
my soft granny bear

who lives beneath the lake
and sings to me . . .
sewing new moccasins,
calling the osprey home.

## Blue Mound

The Sioux rode hard
and piled dark meat
beneath the sunset.

When the smoky skins
filled with moonlight
the dead sang out.

Blue Mound. Grass
and fiery stone, still
greasy with wind.

Below, in all directions,
good land
gutted by tractors.

A sound more terrible
than diesels or dying buffalo
rises like gnats off the prairie,

inflaming the sky.
The farmers plow with radios
wide open.

In all directions
wrinkled arms are gathering
blue dust

into a moonless face . . .
Night with no wind.
There are no songs of this.

# In New Mexico

I remember that camp,
coyotes rooting sagebrush,
mesas of dry blood,
the scorpion beside our fire.

And you knew as well
as I, the ghosts
of cactus and lava
wanted to sleep.

The arroyos were full
of tragic sand, bones
ground by the Padre
in the enormous sunset.

A death chant blew
through us like a black knife,
and we could not answer
that burning well, the abandoned

stones. We could not stake our lives
there, to grind our days
in a bowl of red clay,
without water.

# In Idaho, Going North

The old preacher loved his farm.
His wife ran off with a neighbor boy.
Where has he gone, the man
with good sheep? They say he rode
to the river, they say god knows.

A man's life means so little.
If grass and berries choked his path
his life was good. If he loved,
his hands watered the ground.

This old guy kept the forest.
A clear creek passed his cabin.
There was meadow for the sheep
and meadow for the bear.
Now no man or raven lives here.

Gyppos got it for the timber.
Sheds and log fence caving, they filled the barn
with garbage and chopped down his life.
Ruts and diesel drums in the hayfield—
the land is torn open like a sheep.

The blood runs sour to my hands.
No man's life is long enough
to bring it back, the grass and shadow
of the old man's stubbornness. Turn north,
how deep are the mountains? Who could stay
here?—boil roots through winter, and waken
to see wet slash rotting in the April suns?

# Smoke

What would it be like
to suddenly be surrounded
by fires and icy huts

made of hides and spruce ribs?
To step out of the musty shack
and call graciously

to the tired porcupine, leaving
the door, the salty wood, ajar?
To feel the last word scraped clean

out of the chest cave, a sour bone
carried off by the dogs . . .
Thin smoke feeding silence.

To be called
by many wrinkled hands
and spoken to

in a language of dark sweat.
To sit down with them,
each one packing snow

and flint into burnt hearts.
To find our horses
painted with ashes.

To bathe in hot stones
and braid our blood
for the final camp . . . ?

What would it be?
To watch these clouds redden
like the livers of wolves.

To lie down in moss
with the last caribou, tears
of the raptor going blind.

All the bitter waters
of one life
freezing on the eyelids.

To breathe a song made of frost,
feeling the last note
crushing our shoulders.

To disappear among sooty faces
over the stretched blue hide of dusk,
inhaling the emptiness.

# Under a Black Oak

I found you
dancing at dusk
in a ring of wild iris

calling doves and redtails
into the limestone mountain
until morning

when the laughing ghosts
of Costanoan girls
were rising

from white boulders
in the creek pools
through steaming maple light

black hair wet
to your breasts
down the smoky path

you went with them
to a mound of broken shell
blood and manzanita fire

# A Forge Tune

— for Alex Weygers

He sings the sharp song of a hungry man.
Jigging with sylphs and rusty iron
in a pool of acorns.

Sparks fly off his knuckles, slivers
out of his shoulders, the song
of tight grain and good steel.
The song I want to hear.

The ancient tractor sputters in his fire,
rolled into ash and burning fruit—
lifted like a pomegranate in his tongs!

With each bone hammer new heat, singing a child;
with each quench dance deeper into the raw
stone or hardwood, singing a man—
until a nameless body rises from the stump

in the revolving green light of this
hunger chiselling into his restless shadow—
the song I want to hear.

## Medicine Tree
### —for Georganna

Her chisel smokes with the *contraposto*
of hungers the torque of veins
smoldering beneath our bare feet

winding tendons everywhere
climbing out of pools and stone
braiding a waterfall of green light

out of heartwood and milky grain
of marble she lets go dreamers
and dolphins from her blood

as the madrone reaches
spiraling dark arms
to the hawk floating through mountains

## Arroyo and Boulder

Walking through sage and bunchgrass
inhaling the sprawled out
flesh of you hair of you under my boots
until I realize it's your belly
I am staring at — smoky mound of coals
womb ploughed out of this desert
by the blue horses of a storm
red woman scarred by piñon and cactus
and the births of dancing men
who swallow ashes beneath steel girders
because they can't find their horses
your silence tears my throat
the stretch marks of your body
are full of pollen and the rain
I come to taste

# Framing with You Boy

Beam full of sap and knots
dark eyes we work around
and turn away from the edge
to make it tight
to make it cut straight
against the earth's curving
weather of cries and wings

we screw each syllable down
out of whatever
is vague in our bodies
whatever is smoldering
in our throat roots
out of reach still
each amber slab and trunk sliver
locked into an arrogance of rafters
and studs

and hoisted against whatever
river we think
is turning around us
or without us

our knuckles love this
taste of resin
fog and deadwood hanging
loose in the dripping pines

you know we come here
to notch the big bones
of a place
into place
to light the fire
in our shoulders
until we get it up
plumb

and level now guy
what secrets have we
jacked up
or pried out here
together maybe
and sometimes at a loss

for tools
just hammered something
that scares us
back down
through the pitch rings
and poker chips
into the boozy stump
of our spines

## Rocky Creek Switchback Song

Down the sage and lilac night
through wild cucumber vines
and Spanish moss in oaks
the moon's rusty hook
is still dragging its old bait
above him from one canyon
to the next

Even when wild pigeons
rush back from the whale-turned shore
and morning begins dropping persimmons
at his feet the son of a
coyote can't trick himself out
of his hunger

He hears her sleeping
between the mountains
hears the wet wings opening
beneath wild iris springs and granite
boulders full of milk
and he can't dream himself
out of this thirst

Not even with the obsidian tooth
he stole from Bluebear
to clean these bones he tosses
around the smokehole and the poems
bitten from her black hair

Not even with the poems
while crickets keep sharpening bear teeth
beside the pools
can he outsmart this pain
and catch her
breaking water

He keeps fishing in trees
for the voice she said was his own
four-footed heart smelling home
his own switchback song of the creek
where he thought she swam and hid
between the stones

# *Those Mornings, Big Sur*

Up the canyon, when we dropped
to rest, we could hear the sea breaking,
sometimes a rush of doves.
We were splitting open old buckskin
logs, redwood butts and punkins
handloggers left by the creek
when they went for more booze,
long before a sawlog got winched out of here.
We never heard the dolphins
strangling in the drag nets, we couldn't see
the stain spreading out from the rusty stern,
the horizon turning brown.

                                    Our paths cut down
through Costanoan midden, abalone shell, lupine
and granite dust. We broke an urchin
open on the slippery rock, squeezed a lemon
and sucked the sharp morning from our hands.
On a minus tide it was all there to dig
and pry from the hissing cliff, one swell after
another, before the big plate glass was tilted
up around brass fittings, before the coast
road was oiled slick as another roll of film
and tanker diesels churned the milkshake yellow.

We pumped south of Malpaso Creek for rock fish
or some bawdy wisdom before Hollywood
came and cut the old ranches up
for props. Beyond the little boat
pulling in snapper and cabazone
a barge line was stretching tight

to Japan, but we didn't see it.
Light shattered in the kelp
between our laughing and the big slick
blubber flukes rolling south
out of sight. The blown ridges plunged down
into mist, and the headlands, long and ragged
as a condor's wing, kept curving
out of sight.

        We thought
the seams of the freighters were welded tight,
as we climbed up through coyote bush
to raise our kids in a blaze of redtails.
We believed we could hoist and chink the stones
Jeffers had left grinding below the ocean
drive, thought the trails to our rustic towers
would be too rough for the inspectors, too steep
for the realtors. We couldn't see
the factory ships flushing their bilges,
the old growth forests piled high
on the barge decks, north creeks running red
mud out of clearcuts and smoking craters,
our dream coast hacked and hauled off for sushi
while some country music played
in our cabins, and we believed
our muddy roads would keep out the world.

# II

# *Oversleeping*

Riffles on the eddy
        and aspen leaves breathing
                so early

on my wall—
        look into this
                mirror full of knots

get up
        and wash in the river
                old boy

## Yuh-hai-has-sun

The mountain has black lips
like porcupine and bear
teeth of green ice

in its throat
a salmon burns
and the milk of spruce gathers

from this heart of my mornings
comes the raven
with a syllable of stone

against stone
I have lived
like a juniper root

# *June 6*

Late, wet spring. Now
the valley's bloodshot green,
hot and throbbing
like a great snake.

My brain a bag
of dead mosquitos, my eyes
full of tractor grease,
staring out . . .

Some sheep and a tricycle,
grass and rotting sheds,
the dusty grainfields,
my long day cracking like clay.

Clay I plow and sow for nothing,
brother. You think I'm waiting
for rain? Like the marmot eating a stone
I'm waiting for a fat laugh.

I'm waiting for Bluebear to come down the road
chewing a big wad of fireweed,
dribbling black juice in the dust,
come back for me at last!

## High Water, Catching Roots
—for Bill

We went downstream
rocking in silt
we followed a heron
from bank to bank
barely stroking the shadows
our lines heavy
for once the fish
don't matter the bait
must be gone
long ago those hits
aren't rainbows
they aren't dollies
it's just the bottom
tugging two fools
into a back channel
with both fists
we let go
of the gunnel
cut our snagged lines
to grip the shadow of this
old boat rocking
for twenty years
with laughter

## Stubble

The green silk of the barley field
ripples with a duck call.

I live by a river, barely
awake, barely touching

the mountains. Fireweed and berries
grow between old tractor ruts,

the road winds to a rusty shack
where I have chosen to stay

and turn the pages with my daughters.
One day I cross the river with them

into wings of red cedar and ice falls.
One day I reach back

thanking the clay, barely singing,
covered with green bloodstains

and grease from the mower . . .
Evening, arms full of chaff,

death and sweet clover
ripple the endless dust

of my body,
a dark breeze

like a scythe
passes over me.

## Leaf

Damp arms gather the aching hours
to an eddy, trails through cottonwood
and cedar wind down into a pool

beneath a stump the bears have torn
for grubs. I bend into fall
releasing my hold, humming goodbye

to thick arteries, the long dusk gathering
bearflesh into boulders
under the mountains . . .

My grandmother lives on roots
her dark hand opens in my path
a leaf of old skin, the brown fingers

have woven her song for ravens
and traveled shadows downwind
along the river.

Now heavy wingbeats and the glacier clawing stone
become drops of water swelling
along the veins and drying flesh

and the small bones keep her promise
to October, reaching in silt, opening
the green nights beneath us.

## To a Dead Father

The raven wakes me up
pulling rusty spikes
out of a cold plank

the plank is a road
warped out of clay and moose bone
I have dug

I have cut to the end
of alders to cinch my afternoons
to the wide throb

of the river and cast out
to a ripple
pull the green song

up to me like grandmother's
hands but the line hangs
up in my throat

hooks on some old root
I want to hammer down
to let this life

be like she hummed it
to me hammer it all
back down through my blood

black slivers
through this earth this river
till the story comes back

like a man the acid
in my knuckles in my shoulders
gets hot as fish scales

on a rock so the raven
wakes me up
as I hammer

with a boy's wrists
tightening miles
of barbwire

I chop the road

## Making Wood

Wet morning. The fall
mountains have all bled
into the skin of the birch
I'm splitting. The wood
is honey colored and heavy.

My eyes water in the cold,
so much keeps falling
toward me. The barn
and root cellar are piled full
of all we could pull from the land.
The walls are chinked. Geese calls
bless the river
and the fields,
the shortening days still
high on the banks.

I am ready for winter,
even death,
today.

## Foam

The old logs of the barn
give off a certain odor
of satisfaction, smoke
of musk and mildew.

I have begun to understand
the deep straw, steaming
furrows of daybreak, and my lungs
want the sweetness of jackpine

and manure. My head sweats
against the enormous
flank of one we call
Chuckles, as I listen
to the third stomach

rumbling. I feel an ancient stanza
throbbing through the milk vein
and watch a fist I remember
is mine, these knuckles, cracked palm

and fingers that lead me up rivers
and into them, pull me
to gentle bodies, and deeper
into blue clay and moss shadow,

into the delicate windings of all
blood. Hand moving ahead of me
with strange dedications, almost out
of reach, contracting like some crude

gland of another body.
Milking.

## The Sweater
—for Crystal


You knitted me this
from the mad curls
of our old ram
I can smell your strong hands
in its darkness
I keep moving
inside this wool
like an animal beneath
cold duff and roots
of this mountain no one
ever named it
upriver you whispered
and we knew
it meant lots of berries
here sometimes
I hear your voice
still wanting and still
wet on the stones
wanting to say
be warm

# *Croak*


How many blues have I awakened
to? How many cold shadows am I
swallowing? After a week of snow and wind
I wade into this howling sun.

Light rocks the heavy spruce
and the heavy man!
The gray and sorrel leap
through a buried field
to meet me—How can I
say it? Have I
drunk some blood
with the raven?

## Under January

I sing quietly for the moose
who lies, smoke-eyed, frozen in pain
beside the train tracks.
And tonight, again, for the lynx
draped on a blue snowmobile, leaping
from rigor mortis into a snowy blackness
outside the General Store.

One by one against the numb steel
of Canadian night, the splatter of fur
and wild blood in a man's footprints.
How do I speak to him, hard-jawed
and so restless he has chopped out
a narrow road beyond solitude
or some fear of it? Coffee and whiskey,
what acid chars the mouth and lungs

until a man staggers all winter, turning
his knife in the mountain's throat
for cigarettes and jam, to skin the moon
and hang the snowy fur on some
body blown of glass still gliding
far off through a perfumed lobby?
(And what are *they* drinking to wash down
the anger he went north with?)
Coffee and whiskey, I don't know

how to be straight with him
anymore, or with myself. Neither of us
ever tasted hunger against the trigger.

Something drives a guy to *get some ground*
for himself, stretch and nail a corral
or salted hide beside the river.

By one dirt road or another, we come here
to hurt the wild body open—bleed the trunk,
split the carcass in two, ripping
from crotch to breastbone, taking whatever
we can hold, or imagine we can
keep, like a bright stone or minnow in our fist,
take whatever was ever taken away
before we could remember, or swear, before
we felt the milky lullaby pull away
and we awoke to the smoke of our fathers.
Before we were ever thirsty
or abandoned. We hold the steel

against a blurry darkness, slosh alcohol
into the raw places, split the stump,
and sell the skin. Hammer spring steel
to a slicing feather and quench it,
coil the rope beneath our shoulders,
grind the cowboy tune between our teeth
and fall asleep. We learn how
to quarter animals, sawlogs, and bottom land,
how to abandon, burn the roots, and live alone

beside this river that chews cottonwood
and freezes dark green under January . . .

I touch the lynx and stumble home.
My neighbor laughs a little bit like me.
A blizzard claws the walls
and my guts burn, something hard
and speechless shrinks and tightens
like a stiff hide
around my lungs

Even the little bones I have torn
out of moss or barnyard mud have left
an odor and scar in my palms, one hand
is digging blind for the other
beneath years of homestead snow
and rusty iron. The country is cut up
with one-room lives. How do I
speak with the man upstream
who has chinked himself in between
two stumps? Down river, among my
few cows and a lot of broken steel,
I light a smoky lamp in a single room,
the brown wick curled into a bowl of blood.

## Crystal in the Snowfield

Her back to the afternoon mountains
she goes by a gentle path
to the frozen river, singing softly.

Calling her thirsty animals,
gathering winter shadows
with arms that never

ask for anything. Snow
has drifted over the fence
posts, the narrow road

is buried. Wings of white smoke
trail off the Cariboo peaks.
She crosses the darkening field alone.

You know this woman now, floating
deeper into the blue stillness.
She is not calling you.

## More Wind

Trappers years ago here
would roll over beneath the muskeg
and choke on their snoose
laughing at me, snowshoeing up
from the frozen river
with a typewriter roped to my toboggan
like a moose head!

I keep an axe, some paper and dandelion wine
in my shack above the channel.
But winter has such a bite now
on the place, I can kiss the stove
gobbling birch, still whining like a coyote
with cold nuts. The axe works fine,
but my ink is frozen like a black stone
by the window, fingers numb as horn.

So I pack out with my pitiful gear, spitting
frozen berries into the void, damn near
hysterical with old-timers gone to hell
and their traps—still believing
I've got something to yak about!

## Watering the Stock

There is fog like heavy milk, resinous, lifting
from dark bones of the river,
a morning in my body
without a name.

I don't know these shoulders
drawing water from the frozen ground,
or the sadness of these faces
come to drink.

There is some joy slopping around inside
like a slab of liver or a rock fish,
banging reckless against cold ribs
like well water smacking the cribbing.

Muscle of dumb silt, rising out of breath
like a seal beneath the ice hole, and walking
deeper into blue veins of the mountains . . .
my animals all drinking.

# Coming Home
(after hauling cattle to Edmonton)


One cold night
near Red Pass
my truck quit.

The clear dark
took my brain
with one bite.

I stood
among black spruce
rooted in ice,

the deep
nostrils of winter
pulling me deeper . . .

I awoke
at least once
coming home,

my heart burned
in the throat
of wolves.

# Minus Thirty-Five

As in a birthday
or a fistful of birthdays
clawing my liver
I remember the raven and my cowboy
hat rolled in tractor grease
down miles of windrow and green clay
I am sleepwalking with an oat straw in my teeth
barbwire and bottle of rum
till the sweating fields
tighten like stone
and it is morning

below zero

This is what it means
to be a bag of bones a leathery
two-fisted surprise wobbling upright
on hard ground a skin
pulled over rope and amber spurs
bag of smart pulp hanging
by a corkscrew of smoke
and a red vein
from the sun

I inhale this cold morning
always for the first time
my lungs sparkle
as a tree full of hoarfrost
becomes a huge rose
inside the mountain
light cracks
like a rifle

Tiny white blossoms
on my horse's nostril
and a raven preaching to the emptiness
again

The same raven circles
the clearcut and sinking
cabin at the edge
of more bones and frozen furrows
still stretching
bare beneath me

My short human breath grows
shorter and more human each morning
in this country I have chopped and seeded
this valley that sparkles around and around me
as the blue lung of a glacier
keeps blowing
the raven rises and falls
back and forth from aspen to spruce
croaking some crude proverb
I think I should translate
I think I should get the ink
out of his wings

## Behind the House

The snow farmer sits
in a raw hide, full of smoke
and home brew, barn sluice, bacon
and the laughter of children.
Covered with grain dust and the bitter
harvest his shoulders were stubborn for,
hayseed and frost. The acres of clay
he bet his best days on are frozen
hard as an anvil. His heart
pounds a furrow in the wind . . .
The slab door is open, he is dreaming
into mountains again, squinting
into the empty beak of a raven.
A creature come back to his faith
in potatoes and old shingles
and the ghost who whistles in the outhouse.

# Thank You: Two for My Daughters

(February 7)

Today is not my birthday,
but my daughter has given me
a delicately porous brown fungus
from the wood pile,

wrapped by herself
in typing paper. It is strangely
beautiful, like the lung
of an extinct waterbird,

a gift from the tiniest hand.
Resting on my blank page
it seems huge, like a raw nugget
of some rare ore or gemstone
never known to the Pharoah's jewelers.

(February 10)

Today is my birthday
and my daughters, who have waited,
are so happy.
Colleen gives me a paper
moon and a fish, a bag
of split peas, a postcard
of two deer in three dimension.
She gives me a self-portrait
in blue and red crayon,
a tiny shell.

Aeron gives me
a scrap of leather, a little book
with blank pages, a box
of her used pastels, an eraser,
a sachet for my socks,
a drawing of the spirit
of her dead rat Whitey,
more little shells,
a panoramic in green, blue and red
of our farm, the animals
and the mountains between
their legs. And more animals
cut out of white paper
for me to color.
And they will help.

# Thaw

Like milky blood, pink light drains into the valley,
burning the ridges and blue spines of the forest,
drains into the white fields and white rooms.
The thaw begins, a miraculous ooze from underneath
somewhere, a liquor filling frozen backwaters
of the deep brain, dripping like glycerin into the marrow.
Perhaps it all comes from under the matted hair
of a mammoth sleeping upriver, beyond the glacier
east of here. Perhaps we dreamed too long
against shifting slabs of ice and limestone.
One feels the slow contractions of mountains,
the hands of solitude opening. Blood rises
to the neck and shoulders, the dogs circle
the house. The horses listen and shake off their armor
of ice. The cottonwoods stand still, whispering
nothing. The snowshoes sink. The cows look up
with closed eyes, the raven rolls over.
I swallow my tea and feel it slosh around my kneecap.
The old spruce strokes a little cloud. A heavy tongue
falls from the rafters, and some unfinished pages
sink beneath the crusted river. No one speaks.
No one remembers. We begin to surface
like branches floating into new light, waiting,
believing in blood to come. The moose yawns,
rubbing off grapes of hair and snow, wading out
of willow banks he has chewed all winter.
Birches and poplars glisten with brown sweat
and endless arteries of the sloughs
begin to fill. The snowy peaks rise
like clear eyes watering.

Skin loosens on the walls, the corners seep.
My leather boots unwrinkle and move toward the door.
A deep sound slides from the woodshed.
My bones are thirsty, drunk of salty meat and canned fruit.
My forearms itch. My daughter has found a fly
alive behind the stove!

Steam crawls from chinks in the barn, a smoke
rises from the unsawn log. Under snow piles
the faint creak of iron, a weasel tunneling out
from old bones. The gate swings open a foot, the outhouse
leans over, old boards give up their rusty nails and kiss
quietly in the corners of sheds. The land hardly breathes.
The raven climbs into a spruce top, and curses
like a groggy captain grabbing hold of the tiller.
My smelly clothes roll into a furrow of earth.
The water can clinks.
The jar of salve leaks on the window sill . . .

III

# Man Living on a Side Creek

Rock dust, grain dust, sawdust, early
        sun licking the mountains
                like a bear's tongue, still
some spike of anger in his shoulder.
        Cant-hook, hay-hook, meat-hook,
                always the whiskey breath
rumor of some border—
        some patch of new ground
                or easy timber.

The ruts go west.
        A raven hauls
                morning's smoky hide
over swamp spruce . . .
        the radio scratches
                a partly cloudy day.

Never a girl like mom's sweet potatoes.
        So the shy Saskatchewan boy starts rolling
                smokes early and wanders
from the dugout and bitter fields
        following the greasy harness
                of his dad's last gelding
out of a dead furrow
        and on over the blue summit
                of Alberta
into hemlock darkness, the steep
        green water
                cedar roots and slough grass
winding west . . .

spitting mosquitos and slivers,
                drinking ice melt from a sharp rock
or rye from a cheap label.

He chinks his jackpine shack
        with moss and old underwear
                and traps beaver for tobacco.

The lynx track fills with blood,
        a skinned buck hangs
                from the single-tree.
Never spuds creamy like mother's
        or another God-ploughing man
                made of horse bone
to whip him into the stubble.

The last son stays alone
        on the north side of a side creek.
                When the fur drops or runs out
like the best timber he can poach
        he goes downstream
                to tamp railroad ties
or buck loose hay
        to stay thirsty.

Nothing to do but split the ground
        and backbone with an axe—
                cedar into shakes, clay into barley,
spruce into planks, moose into jerky.
        Nothing to do but smack the country
                like a bitch and keep burning

the veins in his throat
        with booze, because no sweet potatoes
            can open the fist of his father
now, the dead knuckles against his boy's heart
        hard as a tractor sprocket.

Never a woman
        in all the one-room shacks
            with a tin can stove
some rye and a gallon of jam.
        He drags his boiled coffee and smoke
            and tells me about the boy
who ran away—
        so short of breath now,
            coughing and filing to stubs
the teeth of a rusty crosscut
        that he can make cry
            like wind through a prairie woodshed
or the Cree woman in Winnipeg.
        Tales of threshing gangs, Percherons and steam,
            frozen blankets and his mother
in tears, the homestead furrows
        of snow and grief.

My friend knows things I want
        to know, or almost want to,
            so I keep listening
wanting to find the hurt kid inside
        this man leaning in thick sleeves
            jammed at the elbows

trying to grind his loneliness
                into chaff and sawdust, stiff hides
                        and a pot-metal ashtray.
What keeps any man
                living in a single room?
                        Who am I for him? The coffee
is acid, and the old pot warps
                reflections on the table.

I guess he knows I'm thirsty for more
                of the rust and thistles that hammer
                        a gyppo down to his last drink.
He knows I came to stay a while.

 But if I know the taste
                and odor of this place
                        he's burned himself out in,
if I press good steel to the wild
                body I milk and follow
                        to a numb pool
I never knew
                the way he came,
                        that prairie blurring
as he tells it, blurring out
                ahead of the walking plough
                        and the big horse's cracked feet.
I never knew the hands
                of his father, the empty dugout,
                        the bugs banging empty days

and nights. I never knew
        the boy I try to find now
                who stumbled west
with a pain he can't wash down.

So I keep listening. How, if he wasn't
        stooking grain, mom had him
                packing turnips and cabbage
to the cellar, or cranking the separator.
        Finally a blizzard came
                that blew him off to war.
Father's horses got sent off
        to the piss barns, or shipped for fox meat,
                the tractor died
against a cottonwood stump,
        the hay turned black
                in the windrow . . .
Now the rings in every cylinder
        have seized, and nothing
                will fire around here anymore.
"It used to be, hell
        if you had a little spark
                and compression
you were away . . ."

Some crossbred steers
        lick the burnt roots
                around his cabin.
The shake mill rots
        behind a blown-out Ford
                and a heap of bottles.
The last one cut his throat
        and he came home with a battery gizmo
                he holds beneath his chin
to make a voice. The saw won't play
        anymore. The coffee and cobwebs aren't the same.
                So what is there to say
now, when I go there
        for the watery-eyed stories
                I could count on?
The wood stove turns cold, and the radio
        scratches a partly cloudy day.
                A few birch leaves
fall on the tilting porch
        where his thin body leans, and his eyes
                have sunk back to some
storm or furrow
        in Saskatchewan.

Sometimes it is harder
        to reach for another man's hand
                than to bleed an animal.

## Hayfield

The grass is so deep still,
moving under the wind
like the big mare
we could not ride.

Neither she nor this heavy meadow
will come to us again.
They find each other
now, as we had wanted

and together become a wave
at dusk, washing away
from our sheds
and our sorrow

and the wagon tracks
like two warped bones
still sinking
in the sea we chopped open.

# Neighbor Upriver

A shaggy spruce blows its dark
blue wing over a barley field.
The mountain blooms like a purple thistle
behind the farmer wearing a black hat
who grinds and bleaches the day
down to lime and German sausage.

A bear falls out of the cottonwood
and staggers behind the granary,
shot through the ribs.

No stumps anymore. A hog is chewing
the log trapper's shack that is sinking
back to clay, a new barn is choking the sky.
Boots covered with rooster blood.

My good neighbor drove his family
into the bottom land
with an axe and a Bible.
When the last cedar ashes
were harrowed into stubble
he turned his gelding loose in a slough
and left the salty harness for a porcupine.

My devout neighbor keeps his wife
like a sow. She has given him a beautiful
litter of nine. Daughters bend
down long rows of the garden,

dragging dark clouds. Boys with slim arms
pull a last crop off the field
and shovel steer guts into the manure pile,
snickering at the Lord's work and at a stranger
come to buy a heifer or green-feed from their dad.

Winter, a purple sea piles against the barn . . .
Ammonia steam stains the cold morning.
Inside, the cows stand chained in their heat,
swallowing silage, groaning with tons of harvest
bulging the milk vein, filling the gutter.
Calves bawl and stumble in the dark.
The big stainless tank shines like a coffin.

My neighbor has taught me
when to cut grain and rip
open the earth in fall,
how to look at a Holstein's ass.
He doesn't laugh or remember my name,
the bone is thick around his eyes.
He chops at the steep shadows, at the throat
of wolves, and dumps his garbage in the river.
He can smell boards in a tree
like the fat in a goose.

My stomach is full of barbwire
and bear stew, my butcher's tongue
burns like turpentine.
The farmhouse is full of flies,
and I who tuned my fence to the beaver's tooth
am wading downstream with a snag.

When I turn the hell around
my neighbor croaks with a raven's grin,
"Don't you wanna stay here
and fight the elements . . . ?"

There's no shake and goodbye.
Something has thickened his knuckles
till his hand will not open.
He is unloading the silo,
staring at the dull light
of pitchfork tines, a numbness
climbing hardwood grain to his shoulders
where the fear of God throbs like a tractor.

# Spawn

Old spruce    you have drunk
so much silt    blossomed
into cone    and floating shadow
for ravens    turning green water
with bear bones    into cone
dark seed    for two hundred years
feeding crazy squirrels    you
lean out    at the eddy
already so much    given back
to the river    so much root
let go    of the bank
needing to    look down now
see the salmon    roll sideways

## Jackpine
—for W. S. M.


A porcupine has chewed all the bark
and new growth he can reach, climbing
clockwise. I have called
the ghost of an old boatman I love
to swing back and meet me
on the sandbar.

No one comes upriver today.

A blue heron pumps the cool
early light downriver.
The trunk beneath me wobbles
and shifts with your arrival.
It is not clear where the cedars
and the winding smoke of morning
part along the banks,
where your voice begins
or ends . . .

The porcupine covered with pollen
climbs down my spine
into forty some years of acid soil
and needle duff, scratching the salty drum head,
this sooty world stretched over antler and root.
Rubbing his gut slowly over the earth,
he listens for something underneath, chewing
and circling the floor of my cabin,
sniffing leaves and hair, looking

for a door. He hears your fingers
swimming through silences
of stone and charred log,
and he leaves. He knows

there is no place left to stand.
There are no steady planks, the floor
is drifting me out through
webs of autumn skin and willow veins.
This tree is floating upright
like the voice of a well, the throat you
trust and give with a taste
of resin to my mouth, taste
of my own blood becoming smoke
and love again, ripples
of the boatman and heron wings
in the river's light . . .

There is no place to stand still
here, no root to tie up
the boat and the man I remember . . .
From these hours of water
you come back, you take my wrist, and turn
up the palm of my left hand
like the porcupine's belly.

# Canadian Postcard from My Truck

The cottonwoods are beginning to blow
another summer into duck fuzz and smoke.
Clouds boil out of the ice fields
down a river valley of moose meadow and stumps.
Wolf breath hangs above the hay barn.
The muskrat shores are brown.

Following the river, this road
is hacked out with booze and anger
by fists numb as axle hubs, strangers
who leave empty oil drums and pigiron
on the gravel bars when they rip
the last cedar out of its moss.

The tin logging town is hanging
from immense gray ropes
that unwind from the Gulf of Alaska.
Sagebrush bangs a billboard.
A mill stack pumps the sky
full of chlorine.

Horses crowd around the rotting pickup.
A willow grows out of an old tractor tire,
skunk cabbage at the beaver slip.
The highway raven snaps a potato chip
and laughs at the forest ranger.
He laughs at me, grinding south again
to find a black and blue guitar
that will slide between my ribs

because I can't find a tune
to charm these boys.

# *Poplar*

Outside my cabin window, beside the manic red squirrel opening spruce cones, a thick poplar rises from the deep river bank through a soft green blush of willow and cottonwood and straight up through about three thousand feet of blue jade mountain. Its trunk is white with black scars, a knotty column of bone and glacial milk, faintly sooty. A young spruce keeps stroking it with its new growth, but the poplar is vertical and aloof, ready to turn the last trout rings golden before freeze-up.

Smoky shadows crawl down from the frozen lakes, plumes of snow rise from rock faces feeding clouds. I can taste the cold resins of silence. A silty wake winds across the sky, and the road to the headwaters hardens. My mind is tired, but not too heavy to climb this tree.

I have not been here for months. There is still mouse shit in my typewriter, still a pair of long-johns hanging from a spike. There is still, not ten feet from my lamp full of diesel and dead mosquitos, this tall soft-throated poplar rooted motionless in my longest and most precious morning. The handprints of a bear are cut into its smooth skin. Restless boar or wary sow, whoever it was, it has left a clear legend of its climb, a perfect syntax, a clawed cuneiform of its passage.

So I come again to the amber mouth of winter, the last cry of waterbirds, green eyes of the river starting to close. I come back to the near and anonymous language of a black bear in a poplar. An east wind is beginning its dulcimer in the deadwood; smoke from my stove moves up through the bones of light. At last I can reach around this tree with bare hands and empty pockets, my fingers pulling at sapflesh. All of these capillaries are following the bear script, circling upward. All my blood is rising this morning. All of me is wanting again to climb the naked tree and greet the raven who keeps hacking in and out of the void. I am leaving my books and cereal to the squirrel, my axe to the porcupine, and my loose pages to the river.

# Blackwater

If you want to live alone
with lousy fishing, this river
gets plenty wide. Except for a summer
salmon camp, there never were Natives
here. There must have been some good
reason beside the silty water, but he tried
to forget it.

He trailed the moose to a slough,
followed the bear into mist. Up
each side creek he found the same
jackpine cabin empty. No one
stayed, or was coming back. The pools
were empty, the timber too thin.

Country hard for some to make it
is good for a guy whose father ripped clay
prairie open with a team, scalded hogs
with a grin and locked sister down
in the root cellar for smarting up. Good
for anyone who learned your mouth will hurt you.
He kept his anger in his teeth, or plowed it
under with stubble until the ground froze tight.
Before it started to thaw
he was on the dark side of the Rockies.

With a small fire, he holds a few stones
close together, and believes that a life
is listening. By morning the burnt stones scatter
again, almost like faces, out of reach.

You work the bitterness out by going upstream
early. Say it was just good berries
or a buck at the edge of some shadow,
maybe the blue rose of a glacier.

An eagle carves the limestone ridge
half a mile above the muskrat's ripple
where this man turns away from me, or someone
it will always hurt to meet.
His hunger for the mountains
never brings him closer.

# Fall Song

The ripening grain field swells
    out of aspen shadow
        across the river

another river
    sucking silt
        into its wings

and calling geese down
    as all rivers call us
        down from our roads

# IV

# We Went out to Make Hay

1.

We went out to hack open the day like a fat calf or a tree
We went out to rake the earth of mice and low nesting birds
We went out to dig the veins of the black bear
We went out to the meadows that floated like women or low clouds
We startled geese on the sand bars
We went out rolling huge rubber tires, carrying wrenches forged
        from rusted flutes and moose ribs
We went out into the wet arms of dawn while coyotes still called
        over the river
The air was tart as crab apple and cool and the fields rolled
        in their mist, luminous as salmon
        in the first pools of light
We went out while our kids were whispering in their sleep
        like willows above a creek
We went out to taste berries against the barbwire
We went out to make hay
We went out with Jersey cream on our lips, jerky in our pockets
        and bear fat on our boots
Out through the gate as the shores of darkness were sinking
Damp smoke rippled toward us from deer and our cattle
We went out to rub the resins of pine and incense of red cedar
        on our bodies and drink
        the heavy brandy of stumps
We went out to swathe and bale the first flesh of daylight
        pushing our shoulders in circles
        while an eagle scissored the sky
        her flight always changing the borders
        we imagined

We went out with booms and spindles, harrows and seed drills
        choppers and high carbon teeth
        out with hammers and rivets
        and cold meat sandwiches
We went out to cut the long hair of Smohalla's woman where only
        a few wet braids of Shuswap fishermen had been
        camped beside the rack of drying salmon
We listened on the bank by a leaning spruce where Yellowhead
        had watched the slapping beavers
We blew the match a drunk brakeman dropped into the duff
        so the railroad could come through
        and we watched the animals run up side creeks
        with their fur on fire
We went out with marten traps, pitchforks and rum
We rode up Goat River, Castle Creek, The Beaver, Swift Current,
        Horse Creek, Tenmile, Ptarmigan, Buck Creek,
        Slim Creek, the Big and Little Shuswap,
        snapping alders, mud oozing to the girth
        chasing a moose with twin calves
        across the river into black spruce
We went out to skin the lynx and toss barley at the moon
We were thirsty for the liquor of clay and silt, juice of timothy
        bromegrass and clover that swelled
        around our tractor wheels
We drove our horses our tractors our families in circles
        at the foot of Yuh-hai-has-sun
        Mountain of the Spiral Road
We went out to set chokers around the great spruce
        while red squirrels yelled down
        through the hail of cones

We went out to bulldoze the yellow fog between cottonwood
            trunks, and then we hacked up the trunks
            and burned them with diesel and truck tires
When the smoke cleared and the last charred bone was tilled
            under, we admired the harrowed field
            that glistened in the purple silence
            like a great pelt
We cursed and twisted the last roots of bottom land
            into wire rope, worm gears and pork chops
            until the sun was hung like a new carcass
            in a cedar snag
We went out in baseball caps and rubber roles
            and our watches wound tight until they froze
            and fell from our wrists
We went out full of coffee, with latigo leather cinched around
            our stomachs, our hearts full of bacon
            our knuckles like dog teeth
We went out while the smoke from our cabins rose
            straight as a spike
            between the mountains
We went out while the women refilled kettles
            and stirred the coals
            out while they washed Mason jars
            and hung cabbages and cheeses in the cellar
            out while they gathered
            herbs and plucked the chickens
*When will you come back*, they asked, *when do you think
            you might come back*
            the women wondered

We went out to buckle heavy harness on the mountains
        that smelled sweet as lemon
        our lungs big as silos
        our faces red as beef
We went out to find more earth we could drain
        slough we could graze or plow open
We went out to spit blueberry juice at the storm of mosquitos
Sometimes the ripe windrows unwound like lovers
        sometimes like entrails
We went out to the ruts and the breakdowns
        and the coughing animals
We went out for the distance, to look back
        at the peeled logs we had chinked with violence
        the walls we had hewn to keep us
        away from the women
We went out to pump grease into the sprockets
        and kingpin bushings
We went out because it was out and it was endless
        the green day was endless
While salmon crowded to the mouths of clear rivers
        we went out
        we went up the rivers we had named
        and hung them with steel and timber trusses
We put the virgin clay in barges, the new crop in wagons
        the milk of Han Shan's cold mountain
        in stainless tanks
We went out to make hay
We went out without forgiveness
We went out before the raven climbed into his ragged pulpit
        out before the owl digested her weasel

We went out to make wood, to split open birch and red cedar
           we went out for the taste of heartwood
*When are you coming back*, the women whispered, *maybe you*
           *could guess*

2.

We went out to yank the breaking plow down
        through the slough, rolling
        up peat like dark liver
        from under the deep grass
We went out with good steel on our tongues
We went out with barrels of diesel and hydraulic oil
        out with dried fruit and bullets in our trousers
We kept a jug of spring water tied near the drawbar
        a jug of rum or dandelion wine
        stashed in the granary
We went out when the milk was sweet, to crush the green light
        in our fists and mouths
We went out to plow the land we loved in its wildest hours
        as we would have loved our women
We went out to hurt
We went out to cobble and tighten a row of contraptions
        as the glacier began blowing sails into the sun
We went out on the path of Calvin
        and all the storybooks after Cooper
We went out through wild roses and fireweed
        without reading Wang or Walt Whitman
We went out among the nostrils of blue horses
The fields rippled naked and gentle and we went to them
        as we would have gone to our women

We churned ruts to the river, riprapped the banks
             and kept circling the land
             we were burning, stretching
             galvanized wire, driving staples
             even when there was nothing
             to hold
We flushed grouse and rabbits from saskatoon bushes
             and dogwood, slashed and filled gullies
             until they were level enough
             for the mower
We tumbled stumps across the valley
             until no cover was left, no draws
             full of quivering shadow for animals
             to find the river
Before we ran out of ground, before we came to shallow
             water widening in fir darkness
             we opened the throttle
             to hear the last trunks snap like kindling
             under the blade and grousers
When we lit the piles of forest, they hissed
             and cracked, the flames rose
             up the valley, and our smoke
             blew off between the wind chiseled blue peaks
We went out to heap burnt roots, boulders and scrap iron
             into anonymous caves and solitudes
We went to stay out
We tuned our barbwire fences like banjoes
             or sometimes like cellos
             beneath the aspens

We went out to wring the rooster into a dark furrow
We went out to make hay
We went out to shovel potatoes soaked with hog's blood
        out to the sheds where no language is possible
We went out because our male hands trembled when they met
We went out to break our bodies
        while the tractor belched clods
        of diesel smoke into the clear morning
We hauled and hauled on the fields, drunk on alfalfa
        green chop and clover blossom, cries
        of geese and ospreys, sundogs
        and the altitude
We packed and tarped the bunker
        and gloated over the great fermentation
        while a mountain of shit smoked
        beside the milking parlor
Our faces burned raw in the buckshot wind of chaff and straw
        sawdust, sand and grasshoppers
There was always more land coming toward us
        forest and willow bog, breaking like green surf
        in the chaotic sun
        always stones floating up with weeds
        to the surface
We cranked the ropes of the sun around a stump
        and swallowed the river clay
We drove a heavy pipe into the moss of Native dead
        and snickered as it poured
        wheat into the boxcars
We pulled manure wagons into the heat to dump slurry
        on daisies and wild strawberries

We pulled the life up out of the swamps, heavy
        green bladders full of sap and turpentine
        and we punctured them to make hay
Our silage smoldered like sauerkraut, and the cow's udders
        bulged in our hands like bread dough
We baled the sweetness of the deepest land, heaving summer
        upon summer into rotting feed bunks
While the porcupine dozed in a lodgepole
        and the hawk climbed a thermal screw
        we watched our crankcase ink spread
        over the open ground
When the dust of the harvest rose, we watched
        our loaded barns and silos leaning
        into the blurred horizon
We heard the axle snap between our shoulders
        as a storm gathered in the limbs of afternoon

3.

We went out as the saying goes
        with our hearts in our hands
What else can a man do, but go out with whatever he is
        feeling in his hands
        and work it out
Go out to sweat against the tug of high water
        the dark unbroken land
        a little fire in our shoulders
Out, as the Jesus gyppo neighbor says, *to fight the elements*
Red silvers, char and mica, mud and intestines
        the dark sod sliced to ribbons
        the rusty pickup full of barley
        the knuckles numb as roller bearings

Go out to the paddock full of steers, the broken
            iron scattered and sinking
            at the borders, the wet
            lands drained of ducks and seeded
            down to grass, the coyote hung stiff
            on a fence post
Better to stop doubt at the wrists, keep the unspeakable
            stones from climbing up
            the arm veins
Better to stop the hunger at our wrists, and keep desire
            in the fist
Dig to the headwater roots at the face
            of a mountain, under the sledgehammer sun
            twist the rainbow light
            down into a stump
            like a rooster's neck
Go out to the meadows that float like women
            or low clouds, groggy
            with the exhaust of machinery
            out to the ruts and breakdowns
            and coughing animals
Out to the sheds
            where no language
            is possible

4.

We fought muskeg and gophers, shearpins and carburetors
            while a raven was swinging in our shadow
            splitting the air with its sarcastic laugh
            mocking the fever of our need

We went out to squeeze vinegar from devilsclub and thistle
        and we loved the acid on our tongues
We went out to drag the fleece from our ewes and cut
        the balls and horns off our cattle
We went out to make meat
We went out to bleed the animals we milked and loved
        we called them by name
        and threw their hides over the jackpine corral
The air was heavy with pollen and a few slow clouds
        and we went out to taste berries
        against the barbwire
We went out to make hay
While the river was swelling to the mudsills
        our fence rails were already collapsing
        the new borders burning and floating
        away from us
We went out and could not turn back
        until the haymow glowed like honeycomb
        and fire smoldered in the fallow wakes of dusk
We would not turn until the ridges of dust purpled and froze
        against our shoulders, and we remembered
        the laughter of our kids
Not until the tractor sank in the field
        and darkness rippled behind a beaver
        could we remember where the day began
        or think of turning around
The backwater was filling with shadow, and a blue heron
        pulled the barn full of swallows
        downriver toward night

We worked with our backs to the mountains
        waiting for the limestone cliff to crack
        like a wolf's jaw
        the lunar fuse and auroras
        to arc and vibrate subarctic night
Our eyes burned like gasoline to see fall coming
        to watch the alpine whiten
        and push the moose with frost on his horns
        down the mountain
When we could no longer see the flash of the sickle
        or the wake of new hay behind us
When we could just smell only smell what we made
        and taste the cool dusk falling
        on our forearms
We shut off the tractor
        and the river began
        rising toward us

5.

Smell the last honey of cottonwoods
Smell the whole day like steam from a well
        or a fresh stump inside us
Pitch and blood, bodies stained with pulp and juice
        of the day shot through our knuckles
And if we wanted something more, it was too dark now
        to tear it out of the ground

When we stopped burning shafts and ball bearings, pounding
        brass and cast iron, stopped tightening belts
        and roller chains, feeding bales to the mow
        and grain to the hopper
When we stopped making ruts in the earth to make hay
        and there was no more sheet metal to tear
        no more rope or rubber or nerve to fray
We could begin to smell what we made of ourselves
        the heat and mineral of clay
        seed and straw smoldering like a fist in our lungs
        the odor of cattle in our shirts
        the grease and pollen on our hands
We spit into a dead furrow and turned, we watched darkness
        walking up the rifle barrel
We could taste the river on our lips
        and we were thirsty for something
        we could not reach
        or name
We couldn't bang any more out of the ground
        or split open another tree
        it was too late
        to make anything
The river was drinking our land
        drinking the borders we imagined
If we wanted something else, maybe
        we were too tired to know
        or too groggy to ask

Whatever we thought was ours after all
               was not what we went out for
               the old growth ripped open
               green bales crammed to the rafters
               hams hanging in the smokehouse
It was late now, a few geese circled the still water
               and dark fields for the last time
               the heavy basalt wings of mountains
               were folding under the widening night
We turned around, following a tractor rut
               and sagging barbwire to the house
*How hungry are you*
               we could hear them asking

*   *   *

# Glossary and Notes

The Sinker: Navarro Journal, pp. 3–4

*Springboard.* Planks cantilevered from notches in the base of a tree upon which loggers stood while felling the tree.

*Misery whip.* Crosscut saw.

*Coiling rope* and *Cranking the jack.* While timber on level ground was taken out by team or made into "split stuff" (shake blocks, pickets, rails, posts, railroad ties), logs on steep land above rivers were rolled down and floated down to the mills at the river mouths; these slopes were slashed and burned to make all this possible. Rope was sometimes wrapped around the tapered end of logs, so they would roll straight, and loggers carried heavy screw jacks around to roll them free when they got hung up. Green redwood is very heavy, and occasionally logs would sink (thus "sinkers") and stay lodged in the silt until flood currents dislodged them. This logged ground was then farmed, and the stumps burned to keep them from suckering out.

*Steam donkey.* Large steam-powered winches mounted on skids.

*Skidway.* Deck from which logs are canted onto the carriage.

*Dogs.* Steel teeth that secure a log on the carriage.

*Headsaw.* (or *Headrig*). The big, main saw at the mill.

In Idaho, Going North, p. 12

*Gyppo.* A term loosely applied to small, independent loggers working on a dollar-per-volume basis rather than by contract.

Those Mornings, Big Sur, p. 23

*Buckskin.* Logs that have been on the ground enough years for the bark and sapwood to have rotted and to have weathered grayish brown.

*Punkins.* Surprisingly big old-growth logs within easy reach.

More Wind, p. 44

*Snoose.* Chewing tobacco.

Man Living on a Side Creek, pp. 57–62

*Cant-hook.* Log-rolling hand tool, similar to peavy.

*Dead furrow.* In plowing, the last furrow turned, which is "dead" because it doesn't get covered with sod.

*Single-tree.* Cross-piece used with single horse hitch, commonly used for hanging up a carcass.

*Percherons.* One of the more common breeds of draft horse used in the West.

*Stooking.* Shocking grain; stacking sheaves upright in the field for drying.

*Separator.* Cream separator; until recently a common farm appliance.

*Piss barns* (also *mare barns*). Horse urine is used in estrogen production; hence one of the destinations for old draft horses.

*Fox meat.* Slang term for dog food.

Canadian Postcard from My Truck, p. 70

*Pigiron.* Scrap iron.

We Went out to Make Hay, pp. 79–91

*Chokers.* The cable around a log by which it is skidded out of the woods.

*Drawbar.* Bar to which implements are hitched to a tractor.

*Riprap.* To use rock or rubble to prevent washout and erosion.

*Grousers.* Cleats on pads of bulldozer tracks.

*Muskeg.* Swamp.

*Old growth.* First growth; virgin trees.